Against THE Hard Angle

I0884085

ALSO BY MATT ROBINSON

BOOKS

no cage contains a stare that well (ECW Press, 2005)
how we play at it: a list (ECW Press, 2002)
A Ruckus of Awkward Stacking (Insomniac Press, 2000)

CHAPBOOKS

Against the Hard Angle (Greenboathouse Press, 2009)
tracery & interplay (Frog Hollow Press, 2004)

Against the Hard Angle

POEMS

MATT ROBINSON

MISFIT

ECW PRESS

Published by ECW Press
2120 Queen Street East, Suite 200, Toronto, Ontario, Canada M4E 1E2
416.694.3348 / info@ecwpress.com

LIBRARY AND ARCHIVES CANADA CATALOGUING IN PUBLICATION

Robinson, Matt, 1974–
Against the hard angle / Matt Robinson.

Poems.
ISBN 978-1-55022-915-8

I. Title.

PS8585.035172A72 2010 C811'.6 C2009-905968-1

Editor for the press: Michael Holmes / a misFit book
Cover design: David Gee
Author photo: Lyndsay Anderson
Printing: Coach House 1 2 3 4 5

This book is set in Fairfield

The publication of *Against the Hard Angle* has been generously supported by the Canada Council for the Arts, which last year invested $20.1 million in writing and publishing throughout Canada, by the Ontario Arts Council, by the Government of Ontario through the Ontario Book Publishing Tax Credit, by the OMDC Book Fund, an initiative of the Ontario Media Development Corporation, and by the Government of Canada through the Book Publishing Industry Development Program (BPIDP).

Canada Council for the Arts Conseil des Arts du Canada Canada ONTARIO ARTS COUNCIL CONSEIL DES ARTS DE L'ONTAR

PRINTED AND BOUND IN CANADA

ECW PRESS
ecwpress.com

CONTENTS

Demarcation. I feel
The violence of all its delicacy.

— Eric Ormsby, "Coastlines"

I

WHAT THE REST OF US WOULD CALL FALLING

AGAINST THE HARD ANGLE

i. heart

whether to take an axe to this
loose shutter and its insistent clattering,

or not; to draw, perhaps, the hammer back
and drive the bolt into its

place.   whether to cleave.   there is,

no doubt, a force in this — the kind of thing
that bursts barrels and topples

stacks of whatever might not be
nailed tightly down.

whether to simply make our way

over to the door and be done
with it.   to spread our arms; to brace

our shoulders against the hard angle
of the frame — to just make do

right there, standing at the threshold of:

ii. work bench

each rediscovered tool
a recollection

so much less
concerned with its original utility.

become, it seems, another sort

of thing: an object at once
aglow and shadowed,

too, in the stark early morning
of its own

stolid objectiveness, that interrogation

room's bare bulb.
this is pragmatism

varnished thick with coat after coat
of sweat, then tipped

off a table's edge and left to sit

in the damp,
the dark, for god-knows-how-long;

become, despite itself, a fine art
of dust and uselessness.

          don't blink.   each

shuttering eye
moistens the dulling edges of these

newfound saws and chisels, burrs them
with a rust

          that stains the hands.

iii. (flashback: kitchen sink)

leave your apron on the hook
this once.   put the knives away and slide

the block's heft back
into place.

i know the kitchen sink

is full with empties and
a plate from late last night: just leave them

be.   leave the meat
to stew, to simmer; help me tear all the labels

off these

spices and let's — each one of us —
forget a recipe

or two.   pay no attention to
what smells of burning;

let that garlic remain sharply

fingertip slicked —
insinuate itself

into the threads of conversation,
those of your shirt.   don't; don't bother: just

leave the oven on.

iv. stain

your hand a hoe that owns and re-owns the loam
as it crumbles, then slips between

your fingers.   there
are roots and bits of rock in this, unseen

edges and angles that claw sharply back at

your constant reaching.
so, splayed and slick with the effort

you move to wipe your knuckles
clean.   and

it's then, of course, you notice.   the cuticle, ripped back

despite itself, leaks and then
blooms crimson against the stipple stained

surface of your skin.
you pause — time a fist clenched and cocked

there in the air; pause and then

you simply thrust
your hands back down and through the fertile dark,

at the twinge of this new knowledge. you let your hands
till this tiny parcel, quench or staunch

its thirst. you will the stain to simply set.

v. (aside: delay)

            it's become painfully apparent
the airport doesn't have the sweetest clue.

it snores its way through the snowed-in grey
we can see shadowing off

the crack in the dawn of this

morning, each breath.   each breath is a chore,
a burden to be carried awkwardly down

the long hall
of your throat, an oversized frame

of a picture you don't really care for.   your arms:

they simply can't stretch far
enough; you are always on edges.   and the frowns

people wear as they shuffle about
are only spun tire tracks

mirrored: the sullen discomforts

of their shifting stark roads now
brow-etched across them through the windows of earlier cabs.

    this, we might say,
is the difficult face of travel.

the taut, weathered skin of the tent

in which anger lies fitfully sleeping.   but
the rules here, we all know, are still

different: you keep your baggage close by at *all* times.
no more than an arm's length

away; no

exceptions.   and as bad as this seems,
we can guess

our alternative's both nothing *and* something
like love, only instant.   so: having thought, you think

you should sit and be glad for the crowd

of mismatched totes crashed at your feet, how much
you still have to be carted about.   be glad

for this time — this new time —
you've been gifted to consider just where you might've been

going; to rethink that blown out of proportion.

vi. apophatic

the milk — gone off.   just
then: as it clots past

the lips and hits the tongue's tip.
        her breath,

the morning after.

                your head, circa
then.   a good wine left

uncorked on the counter,
overnight.   and: the not knowing that.

        endings

of good movies; the beginnings
of the not-*quite*-bad-enough

ones, in hindsight.
        the milk, so close to its date

you can't bring yourself

to venture a taste, can't chance
bringing it close to your lips.

that carton left to sit
on the counter: the absence of even the possibility

of something rotten —

vii. metamorphic

the moments recollected
are stones

childishly hoarded
in pockets,

then left to themselves and

their shadows,
their constant knocking

and wear.
                    a heavy lint,

defeating itself.

            and we are
not, have never been, geologists —

know nothing but simply
how rough

or how round each feels

in the closed book of a hand;
how another — left out on the sill

— still
impossibly holds the day's heat

hours after.

viii. (flashback: a holiday offering)

let me say this much,
he says:

i have nothing here to offer you
this christmas;

nothing but

the now blooming pulse
of what

we've known
this year as it leaks —

smashed

bottle-spilt — from the heel
of my left hand.

            my tongue —
a fist — is heavy with this

salt gift,

with the heft of knowing that it is
at once both

all too much and so clearly
not

enough.

ix. (an other's perspective:
they dance around the issue)

to call it a pause is not
quite right.   it's simply a moment

drawn out and snapped
tight, so taut

as to cut this thick air

like soft cheese
in the midst of a stale cocktail party.

                    and time, nearly
spraining a ligament, bends at the knees;

a drunk's genuflection, or

stumbling ease with
what the rest of us would call

falling.   and they reach for it
then — like

a chalked twine they'd thought

tied — in the hope
of some demarcation.   the lie?   they

know it now, know it
all too well, as the narrative line of

a necessary fiction.

x. (flashforward: table & chairs; set)

the legs coffeed
and cut out from underneath that first

kitchen table
we'd bought, online.   unfinished, then,

i've since somewhere near-half re-done this

old thing
of ours: measured and re-measured; hacked

away until i could
put my feet up.   ask any carpenter: no varnish holds

against that many bottle bottoms.   there is

always, as we know, a tipping point.
and i'm still careless

with my feet.   the matching set of chairs
are still

just as unfinished as the newspapers we'd planned

to set underneath as we painted and sealed
the things.   believe me.

believe me when i venture there is nowhere
not too rough

to the touch

to sit.   were anyone to run a finger, a palm,
along this edge

they'd feel the grain
announce itself, implacable: another long-term trick of time

and moistures.

xi. heart; murmur

whether to simply make
our way over to the door and be done

with it.
(of the frame — to just make do

right there, standing

at the threshold of?)
there is, no doubt, a force in this —

the kind of thing that bursts barrels and topples
stacks

of whatever might not be nailed tightly down.

whether to cleave.

whether to take an axe to this

loose shutter

and its insistent clattering, or not;

to draw, perhaps, the hammer back

and drive the bolt into

its place.

to spread our arms; to brace our shoulders against

the hard angle.

IT'S NOW,
HE THINKS,
WE LIE
IN IT

you've phoned, after years; long
distance, mere months
'til our papers are stamped & folded &
filed, & asked — yes, asked — for this,
too.   for, more or less,

the old bed.   so now it's the mattress
as understatement, as a less legible diary
of union, its traceries now fold-faded & worn into
some labyrinthine dreamed detritus, a world of un-sprung
coils & dust & mites & such.

don't you agree? you know how
loss can be felt, only slightly; how it winds around &
into itself, supports its own
precarious weight, all in spite of.   everything
serving as frame.   & how

we notice this only — every once
in a while — when we shift in some way, often just
as we swallow that last mouthful of the meal
of a day. as we turn our heads toward the dark, toward
the shadow that

an eyelid spills just then. gist; then. just:

QUARTER-YEAR TRIPTYCH

i. january; storm

and the city? it seems

abashed, its face gone near purely

white, with the knowledge of what we know

(of love). the sky, too, it seems

is heavy with this, with us, with

lazy mornings and those languid moments

before the eyes give in, finally, to sleep.

each ticker-taping flake

that falls — that worries its way to

the ground — is simply a moment gone

crystal, held briefly static in near-zeroed air.

in this way the snow is a fleeting

warning; a sudden crisp augury:

the season's vertiginous manner of telling

us to steel ourselves to the cool

elemental, to starch each concise beauty against

the wrinkling rip of the wind as we puzzle

our way down or through. to

both splay the arms as wide as they stretch and

then, vice-like, hold — hold dear

what we have, what we have taken in.

ii. february; song

think.   think waking.

those first fissile splits of eyes' lids as they crack

the shell of the day.   and the hands

with nowhere to go, no real use but

the simple accenting of absence; an artful matting

of canvas left blank in its frame.

you *could* say each finger's tip

is a bright sulphurous match struck against the mute

charcoalish dark of an abandoned alley

at night; a flame bursting the panorama of

naught into brief, brilliant view.

think, perhaps: morning's stretch as half-hearted

semaphore, a flaccid flagging of loss.   or even:

the arms themselves extraneous —

the wings of a flightless species of bird, one

no one has yet bothered

to name, to hunt.   because, despite our best

efforts, there's no exact definition — no

easy shorthand — for this.   there is only, it seems,

a crude mathematics,

that estimation — a circumferential logic of arms.

iii. march; tracery

to know want

as an additional sense? it's to have traced

and re-traced the fine line between

waking and dream along the curve of her

spine. to have known you'd worry

the bone braille of that

near indecipherable code

until your fingertips and their prints were nothing

but memory worn raw and wine red —

a fine, antiqued ache you could hold and sip

slowly, hours after. yes:

to want and to want and to want

in this way is to run one's lips over

the hard salt fact of each thought

again and again in the carved dark of the night.

it's to know each sense

as additional want, each breath as a new chance

to choke on

the crook of a smile. your tongue

left as nothing, if not in the way.

useless, in fact, as you swallow the day.

II

TOEING THE SLACK-ROPED NARROWS

ROTARY; ROUNDABOUT

Armdale Traffic Circle (Old Armdale Rotary) — Halifax, NS

they've gone, it would seem; gone and
changed the rules.   what we thought we knew, falling
in on itself. all feral
centripetal.   the old rotary has gone roundabout;
given in.
and this change, you might think, this
new line of thought — if you were
to spy it all from a distance — is getting us nowhere.
it's only a constant worrying
of old blacktop blanketed snug by some new; a circular
logic.   squint-seen, it's performance,
suggestion — a suggestion of some sleight-of-hand
here at the tip of the arm: the near
magical pull of some deep-seeded magnet now spinning,
we'd guess, completely
and fully out of control — a crazed, elemental
ballet.   so many iron filings in constant pirouette.
and it all only skirting
the crux of an issue.   or, perhaps, this is
simply and only some city planner's end-of-week desktop
playing-at-god, asphalt parable.   just more
arcane lines and lessons. about waiting
one's turn.   about turning corners; about
the slowly arced knowledge of some concept we've come, over
time, to call patience.

HISTORIC PROPERTIES & THE LIKE

                    one more beer, you think.   and
through the nearest pane of glass

the buildings, now torn
down, salt their silhouettes across what would've been

adjoining walls like catches of fish once fresh
and slapped onto the docks

but left to rot their way into
the memory's salt-sketched version of impermanence,

that sickly sweet paradox.   she's gone,
you know that now, and not

likely coming back.   so you throw that worn fact down your throat
and work your neck; finger

the newly minted map of this,
your sweat-stained shirt, and trace your way through

time.   brick by sun-scarred brick
you hack and swallow,

run your tongue along this cobble.

GRAND PARADE, HALIFAX

'the square is the only major shape that is man-made'

a pause, of sorts.   a rupture in the stolid brick
& concrete rote
that is the city's downtown counting;
our stepped caesura.
          it has been here — we have been
here — for the tumult & explosion of the core, its people.
          a frenetic foreign chaos
of debris.   we have been right here & shuffled
the icy restlessness of near-zeroed november
mornings & — mindless — kicked
at what's been cobbled,
together.   we have been
here — just some of us — a slight
bit drunk. loose-shouldered & slack-jawed, searching
the night's unsteady dark for a fight, for
a bite of salty meat or slice
of pizza.   we have been here, however briefly,
on the way: up, or down, or over.
we have been here; we have been.
          we have, at very least,
just this: a near accidental architecture of moments.

CITADEL HILL

Citadel Hill National Historic Site — Halifax, NS

the elephant, you
might say, in the room.   or, that hulking, hillocky
older kid — clad all in the kitschy, just
just-past style
hand-me-down trappings of a brother who's long since left
home, this town.   and how he stands
there, here, in the eye of the storm, with recess
hub-bubbing each and every which way around him; and him,
slope stoic, seeming oblivious.   a languid
precursor of force, a loose laundry pile — all folds
and tumbles and grass stain — of slow-twitch muscle,
unused.
a mountain of gaze.   how, like clock-work,
he'll shuffle and spit, hock thunderous.
how he never forgets.
in the end, though, it's how he looks.   looks:
down, and over, and out.

SEA WALL, YORK REDOUBT

You like it under the trees in autumn,
Because everything is half dead.
— "The Motive for Metaphor," Wallace Stevens

                                        i like this place, now, in its muddy march
renewal, because it is agreeable — because in its sopping
confusion of footprints
i am free to stumble and not recognize my doing so,

in hindsight.   but, i also appreciate the willingness
of these remnants of the wars,
of struggles greater than mine, to align themselves —
in the midst of their own haphazard tumbling

and collapse — with something
akin to my grief; to allow it something of the concrete.
                  and the cooperation of this weather,
of the harbour's incessant crashing and its rock-spit? it *is* a sort of liquid

kinship — a coupling and mingling that,
while not at all surprising given the cycles, the multiplicity of water,
is a sympathetic sort of storming; a tipped glass.
                  indeed, that everything here is fully dead,

or seems to be — only the cracked, dark
spruce hint at growth, at life — is helpful, too, if only by suggestion,
as, through previous experience, i know that even this
dun, salt-beaten concrete is split wide by greens in spring.

PERHAPS YOU CAN'T GO HOME AGAIN

The Dingle (Sir Sanford Fleming Park) — Halifax, NS

standard: briefly, upon a time, once, we were —
we suspect, we guess — amazed.   but now, we're sure,
the park's stone entryway fails fully
to impress; upon further inspection is, we might now suggest, nothing
but a small, lopsided cobble framing an asphalt-grey
tongue's splay; some awkward uncle's wry party smile after
one too many gin.   even the scattered
smattering of metal gates slalomed further down the drive, just
off the winding road — those thresholds nearly hidden at the ends of
our tree-studded high school lovers' lanes, those underpinnings
of each re-repeated conquest — are, in this day's light, a slight
letdown, a disappointment. each season's paint, the uneven slopped
green coats, just the ruddy, pock-marked cheeks
of some sudden sidewalk-seen faux starlet whose skin, up close,
has gone to pot from day after day of too much foundation, too much
exposure to the bright, brusque honesty
of stage lights, of performance.   in fact, a closer look would
show these aging welds rust buttered; seaming. a briefly outstretched hand
would find the old lock boxes suspect, lichen moist, near
seeping; the simple roads we'd guessed we took once, now a maze.

THE OLD BRIDGE

Angus L. MacDonald Bridge — Halifax – Dartmouth, NS

how we get there
from here, or, vice-versa.   city's signature, writ large –
all old boy flourish & ponce.   everyone,
riveted.   green monster, horned.
a drawn bow, arrowing
skyward.   some poor man's amusement
park ride; flaccid coaster.
(grid-locked at dusk, mid-deck's the apex of some harbour-
sunk ferris wheel, the view all
carnival: dark puddle & sparkle & glitz.)   a suicide's fix.
should moon, fog conspire — it's low-slung
constellation, at night.   look,
from just past the basin, our eyes are high-wire, blown pupil,
acrobats toeing the slack-roped narrows
atlantic-ward; the span a drunken parabola, a grand balance pole.
it's innocence, lost;
the steely slow arc of knowing, of coming across
some unwanted knowledge.   disbelief,
its path.   the suspension of just that. that toll.

INLAND, FROM THE OCEAN

VIA Rail Station; The Ocean Line — Halifax, NS, to Montreal, QC

leaving. the afternoon
is hot, is thick with it — this smutch of breath.
passengers
gather, a paned condensation by departure
gates, by windows. bags rasp, clasp-cough across the tile
floor, its subtle ruts. as our time
approaches, tide-like,
an order develops, redevelops; wears the once-crisp edges of this
leaving; leaving us dulled and sullen.
later, in motion, the window
is a charcoal or pencil sketch, smudged; a concrete newsprint
stuttered all along with a ragged stitch
of power pole Ts: repetitive, unsteady —
a grade-school printing exercise. somewhere
before bathurst we are a drive-by theatre; we are a travelling
circus, mid-way. an old man, a buick,
a mother, two kids: soda pop sticky with summer, people
stare and wave themselves away. after
coffee, the drummondville morning
is workmanlike; a grass stain on faded denim. on approach,
montreal is a spilt pallet:
so many cardboard boxes, bleaching in the sun.

STUDY: WILLOW TREE, TRAFFIC

Stalled car at rush hour; The Willow Tree Intersection — Halifax, NS

rush hour.   this
quid pro quo halt and jerk, rigmarole
syntax of entrance and exit, side- and rear-
mirror-viewed fracas of coming and going —
all mufflerhuff shuffling
and impatient clutch tap.   gap control
maintenance.   brake and back
pedaling.   just ahead,
there's some sudden shift, something
stuttered.   an un-(*for-chrissakes*)-intended
caesura.   our tempo slurs, slowed;
stalled. a ford, flooded — four-ways aflutter, all
tachycardiac, all strobe frantic with the sudden
unease of seized piston; all too hot with some hood-hidden bother,
with this abrupt end stop. this cemented
enjambment.   (you'll note:
squeegee kids hover, still; vulture curbwise, picaresque. not
everything's failing to scan.)

PUBLIC GARDENS, POST-STORM

The Halifax Public Gardens — Halifax, NS

the aftermath,
a mess.   a sprain-splayed

algebraic of wind-knocked

stems and
stocks, this carnaged leaving, this scatter

of scrawled 1s and 2s, rag-

dolled Xs and drunk-stumbled Ys.
some hastily

figured storm sum; real roots

exposed.   a wrought- framed
proof.

a fraction reduced.

TERMINAL

Halifax Ferry Terminal on approach from Dartmouth — Halifax, NS

a safe bet, on approach.   to wager this harbour-viewed silhouette
as an *unintended* likeness.   as happenstance,
mere chance resemblance. as a midday
flight of fancy; as too much commuted
coffee, playing tricks.   we *know* anything
more than the suggestion of some near-ironic accident — of design;
of budgets, of neglect — stretches the bounds of credibility.
sends them, flung far and soaring, out the window. disappears them
into thinnest air.
                                        nonetheless, we have — ferried through
these cabin windows, seen from the deck — this; portent. an arthritic —
steel and vestigial rust — gull, pier poised.   caught ungainly
in the white-capped harbour-chop; in,
perhaps, flight and strike's conjunctive moment, its inverse instant.
                    and the terminal, we're sure now,
glowers — all wingspan and noon-sun
shadow — as we bob and thrum our way
from dartmouth to the shore, closer inspection.   and after
some reflection, it's as if we've been tide-drawn to a bird so close to death
its scaffolded rigour, its rigid auduboned semaphore, is
as natural as any posture.
                                        so then: docked and rising from our seats,
we think we better apprehend the subtly violent undercurrents
in our arrivals, our departures; know the ebb
and flow of some slowly building menace.
                    we step off and into our foreboding become architecture.
we choose flight, having landed.

THE NEW BRIDGE, RECONSIDERED

A. Murray MacKay Bridge — Halifax – Dartmouth, NS

is once removed.

is stevens' inverse, exponential.   *not* the thing itself, but ideas of
the idea of the thing. of itself.

is the *just-now* tasted sour, green, apple-doll face of the fist-crumpled
twenties you snatched from that dresser-left purse for a six-pack, or two.

is what's burning that hole in your pocket.

is the last sip of something; your medicine.

is a line.

is in the midst of telling lies straight to your face, fingers a secreted
lattice; that unseen insurance.

is our cleaving.

is each sleepless night you spent thinking of just how to leave her; your
brow, your eyes each next morning.

is some headaches.

is the near usurious price we've paid on our way over or through; the rattle and clang of loose change falling away and against itself.

is oil and water; a good vinaigrette.

is ten days off school for that one epic punch in the face, its cheek kneading like dough on your knuckles; the bruise's refusal to bloom, right away.

is three quarters.

is old butcher's twine, cut precisely to length, strung and then bowed; cinched at the tip of your now-numbing finger, its pointing. how it pales.

is a post-it note fallen, tucked under the fridge. how it's swept into sight.

is what you felt — you think — over beers, that one night.

is a long distance phone call's split-second between ring and "hello?"; that frantic fissility, that hard-charged space.

is what's cleft us.

LAST CALL AT THE MIDTOWN

Midtown Tavern and Grill Ltd — Grafton Street, Halifax, NS

this, our last hour of loose lips and spills
scarcely noted by anything other
than some faux-florid fingering — hand-slurred
slapdashery — of an air gravy-humid
and stale with steak, with
sweat.   we nod.   eye
contact a contract, an order placed, here.
                    look: these slicked hops slosh; skip, jump
and then crest the false
dykes of our flourished half pints
with each tabled fist that smack gavels these
spill-shellacked arborites, those tipsy
chipped edges our now-buckled knees will soon know
are slump-lumbered and
resting on *near* even legs.   a toast. a toast!
(we order in twos; hands arc the deluge.)

THE GRAIN ELEVATORS

The Halifax Grain Elevators Limited — Corner of South Bland & Atlantic, Halifax, NS

some context, perhaps.   trains — *less frequent,*
we're told — clatter and rumble, nearby.   there
are ships. nights, passing.   and just down
from what once was a peeler bar just down the road — torn down
now, years back — we have this.   industry's crumbling
veneer.   these cocked, clenched fists — these grain elevators —
near assaulting the asphalt, the gravel
and lost soul shopping cart mess,
that clutters the corner of south bland and atlantic.   the atlantic
harbouring grudges, beyond.
the insensitive heft of it all.   massive,
each weathered bone column, each concrete finger: all tendon-tensed
against impact, near white-knuckled
to breakage.   time was, you could count on a body
or two, an old car.

you might say this is not unlike how a love turns —
how that looks, over time.   how it becomes
weathered and pock-marked; a remnant of effort all scribbled and tagged
by long nights, passers-by.   becomes
argument as foundation; becomes
all-(*it would seem*)-of a sudden some concrete conundrum.
each day a bare-boned utility.
how this all leaves us wearied,
worried; stress-fractured and cracked like this dun-dull brute tonnage,
new weeds sprung up at our base.   silos cemented in place.
so, stuck, we look down: scan the dust
and blown trash. we sift through what's fallen, what
we guess has been spilt.   let it run past our fingers, ghost
through the new fissures of loosely cupped hands.   all those fine
grains salting the air, a coarse grit caught at the back of the throat.

ACKNOWLEDGEMENTS

Earlier versions of some poems in this collection have appeared in the following publications (many thanks are extended to the editors): *The Antigonish Review*, *Northern Poetry Review*, *CV2*, *The Malahat Review*, *Grain*, *Prism International*, and *The Fiddlehead*.

The following poems have also appeared previously as limited edition Gaspereau Press broadsides: "heart," "table & chairs; set" and "rotary; roundabout."

An earlier version of the long poem sequence "against the hard angle" won *The Malahat Review* Long Poem Prize in 2009.

An earlier version of "against the hard angle" appeared as a limited edition, letter-pressed chapbook by Vernon, BC's Greenboathouse Press. Thanks to Jason Dewinetz for his beautiful presentation of the poems, not to mention the keen editorial advice.

A version of "grand parade, Halifax" is exhibited on a traffic control box in Halifax's Grand Parade as the inaugural instance of the inclusion of poetry in the HRM's Art in Public Places Program. Thanks to Heather MacLeod for allowing me to be involved in that program.

Many thanks are also due to the fine folks at ECW Press. This is especially true with regard to Michael Holmes, my editor, whose attentive reading of the poems and insightful suggestions for the betterment of them were, and still are, greatly appreciated.